Fashion
Mode
мода

1500-1954

L'Aventurine

Introduction

A collection of historic fashion illustrations can serve various purposes: portray the tastes of a certain period, present a selection of exquisite original prints, describe a bygone era, and provide departure points for readers interested in exploring the world of fashion. This volume includes several extraordinary examples of the ways 19th century and 20th century fashion was depicted. In addition to briefly covering 16th century fashion, the book also examines styles which to our eyes appear frankly picturesque rather than elegant.

The bulk of the illustrations was gathered from magazines and advertising material in which setting, graphic handling and illustrative style combine to enhance the charm the model would evoke in the viewer. Through the depiction of staged scenes from life (children playing, women immersed in conversation, moments of relaxation) 19th century illustrators created an image of their time. In the illustrations from recent periods, however, one can note the use of a more stylized, perhaps more practical design, where the model is often portrayed with allusions to the physical characteristics of famed film stars, somehow detached from reality, removed to another world, and suspended in motionless beauty. What is most striking in these illustrations is the clothing, the folds and colors of the fabrics, whereas in the earlier plates the modern viewer is drawn to the models' faces and the tableaux the figures fill with their physical presence.

More so than other art forms, fashion has changed the ways it expresses itself. Witnesses to this evolution are the images fashion uses to create our contemporary collective imagination-beauty displayed, polished and shined.

To gain a different perspective, the reader is invited to journey back to a past world of elegant gowns and *grandes dames*, hinted smiles and shy damsels.

Introduction

Une compilation de dessins de mode peut avoir plusieurs buts : montrer des costumes anciens, rassembler des illustrations magnifiques, faire revivre un monde disparu ou proposer des idées et nourrir la réflexion des stylistes. Ce livre présente des exemples significatifs de la façon dont la mode se présentait et s'imaginait entre le XIXᵉ siècle et les années 1950, ainsi qu'une petite parenthèse consacrée au XVIᵉ siècle et à une façon de s'habiller qui, de nos jours, parait plus pittoresque qu'élégante.

Les images proposées au lecteur proviennent surtout de revues ou de documents publicitaires dans lesquels l'atmosphère, le graphisme et le style contribuent à rendre plus séduisant le modèle présenté. Les scènes reproduites (avec des enfants qui jouent, des dames faisant la conversation ou se divertissant) sont typiques de la façon dont le XIXᵉ siècle créait sa propre image. Dans les illustrations plus récentes, on peut cependant remarquer un changement, un dessin plus stylisé que l'on pourrait qualifier de plus « pratique », dans lequel le modèle reprend les caractéristiques des représentations d'acteurs de cinéma, se montre éloigné de la réalité, immergé dans un autre monde, figé dans sa beauté immobile. Le plus étonnant dans ces illustrations, ce sont les costumes, les plis et les couleurs des tissus, alors que dans les images plus anciennes, l'œil se sent attiré surtout par les portraits et les scènes qui représentent des personnages et rendent leur présence physique.

La mode, plus que tout autre art, a changé de façon de communiquer. Il suffit de penser aux représentations qui, de nos jours, nourrissent l'imaginaire collectif à travers une beauté éclatante et irradiante.

Pour avoir un point de vue différent, le lecteur est invité à faire un voyage dans le temps, dans le monde de l'élégance, des grandes dames et des demoiselles timides et pudiques.

Einleitung

Eine Kompilation von Modezeichnungen kann mehrere Ziele bezwecken. Zum einen stellt sie eine großartige Sammlung von Originalillustrationen zusammen; sie macht uns mit Kleidung vergangener Zeiten bekannt und lässt somit Verschwundenes wieder aufleben. Zum anderen möchte sie Anregungen geben, Ideen vermitteln und Reflexionen von Designern und Stylisten nähren.

Dieses vorliegende Buch präsentiert außergewöhnliche Beispiele der Modewelt, wie sie sich selbst sah und darstellte von Beginn des 19. Jahrhunderts bis hin zu den 50iger Jahren des 20. Jahrhunderts. Des weiteren wird ein kleines Kapitel dem 16. Jahrhundert und seiner Art sich zu kleiden gewidmet, was uns in der heutigen Zeit wohl mehr pittoresk als elegant erscheint. Die dem Leser vorgeschlagenen Bilder stammen insbesondere aus Zeitschriften oder Werbedokumenten in denen Graphik und Stil eine Atmosphäre schaffen, welche das vorgestellte Modell äußerst verführerisch erscheinen lassen.

Reproduzierte Szenen, wie spielende Kinder, Konversation haltende Damen oder sich anderweitig unterhaltsam vergnügende Frauen, sind in ihrer Art und Weise typisch für das 19. Jahrhundert, welches sich somit sein eigenes Bild schuf. In den neueren Illustrationen wird man jedoch eine stilistische Veränderung in den Zeichnungen wahrnehmen. Die abgebildeten Modelle repräsentieren die aus der Praxis entnommenen charakteristische Züge wie Filmschauspieler, sie zeigen sich weit von der Wirklichkeit entfernt, eingetaucht in eine andere Welt und unveränderlich in ihrer beweglosen Schönheit.

Das Erstaunlichste in diesen Illustrationen sind die Kleidungen selbst mit ihren Falten und Farben, während dessen man sich in den älteren Abbildungen durch deren Porträts und Szenen angezogen fühlt, lassen sie doch die dargestellten Personen durch eine gewisse physische Präsenz herausheben. Die Mode hat, mehr als jede andere Kunst, die Art und Weise der Kommunikation beeinflusst und verändert. Es reicht an Abbildungen oder Darstellungen zu denken, welche uns, und das bis in unsere heutigen Tage, durch ihre kollektive Imagination nähren und mit ihrer strahlenden Schönheit durchdringen. Der Leser ist eingeladen sich eine eigene Meinung zu bilden und sich auf die Reise zu begeben in die Welt der Eleganz, nobler Damen und scheuen und schamhaften Fräuleins.

Предисловие

Настоящее собрание исторических иллюстраций, посвященных моде, представляет собой сборник подлинных изысканных гравюр, дающих возможность читателю ознакомиться со вкусами европейцев в период от 16-го до 20-х веков. Мы надеемся, что представленные иллюстрации позволят некоторым образом охарактеризовать прошедшие эпохи и дадут отправную точку для желающих открыть мир моды. В добавлении к краткому обзору моды 16-го века, в книге детально рассматриваются образцы моды 19-го и 20-х веков, преимущественно на примере французских и итальянских мастеров. В издании также приведены стили, которые на наш взгляд являются черезчур яркими, что лишает их некоторой изысканности и изящества, но не сколько не умаляет их красоты.

Основная масса иллюстраций, взятых из журналов и рекламных проспектов, скомбинирована таким образом, чтобы передать колорит времени и вызвать восхищение зрителя. Через отображение сцен из жизни - играющих детей, женщин, поглощенных беседой, моментов отдыха - иллюстрации 19-го и 20-го веков создают образ времени. В современных рисунках можно заметить использование более стилизованного, более практичного дизайна, где «модель» всегда изображается с намеком на черты знаменитых кинозвезд, каким-то образом вырванных из реальности и перенесенных совершенно в иной мир и там оставленных в своей неподвижной красоте. И что самое поразительное, изображение одежды, складок и цветов тканей на гравюрах делает нарисованные модели живыми.

Так же как и многие другие виды искусства, мода постоянно меняет свое самовыражение.

Чтобы перед читателем открылась необычная перспектива, ему предлагается «отправиться» в прошлое, в мир элегантных людей и благородных дам, загадочных улыбок и скромных девушек.

Contents • Sommaire • Inhalt• Оглавление

1500

CITTADINI.

Etching, 16th century

Gravure, XVIᵉ siècle

Radierung, 16. Jh.

Гравюра, 16 век

CONTADINA.

Etching, 16th century

Gravure, XVIᵉ siècle

Radierung, 16. Jh.

Гравюра, 16 век

CONTA- DINO.

Etching, 16th century

Gravure, XVIᵉ siècle

Radierung, 16. Jh.

Гравюра, 16 век

DONNE MEDIOCRE.

DONZELLA NOBILE FVOR DI CASA

Etching, 16th century

Gravure, XVIe siècle

Radierung, 16. Jh.

Гравюра, 16 век

HVOMO NOBILE.

Etching, 16th century

Gravure, XVIᵉ siècle

Radierung, 16. Jh.

Гравюра, 16 век

NOBILE ORNATA.

Etching, 16th century

Gravure, XVIe siècle

Radierung, 16. Jh.

Гравюра, 16 век

HORTOLANE.

Etching, 16th century

Gravure, XVIᵉ siècle.

Radierung, 16. Jh.

Гравюра, 16 век

1812

1820

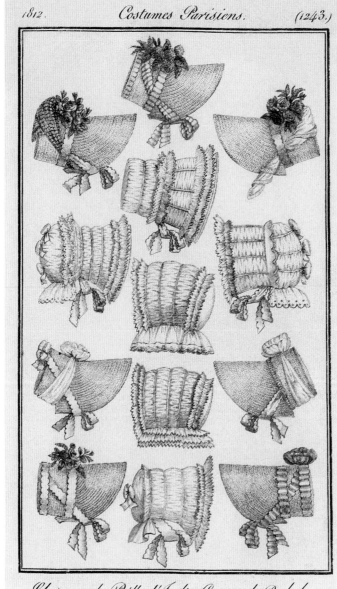

1812. *Costumes Parisiens.* *(1243.)*

Chapeaux de Paille d'Italie. Capotes de Perkale.

Etching, 1812

Gravure, 1812

Radierung, 1812

Гравюра, Париж, 1812

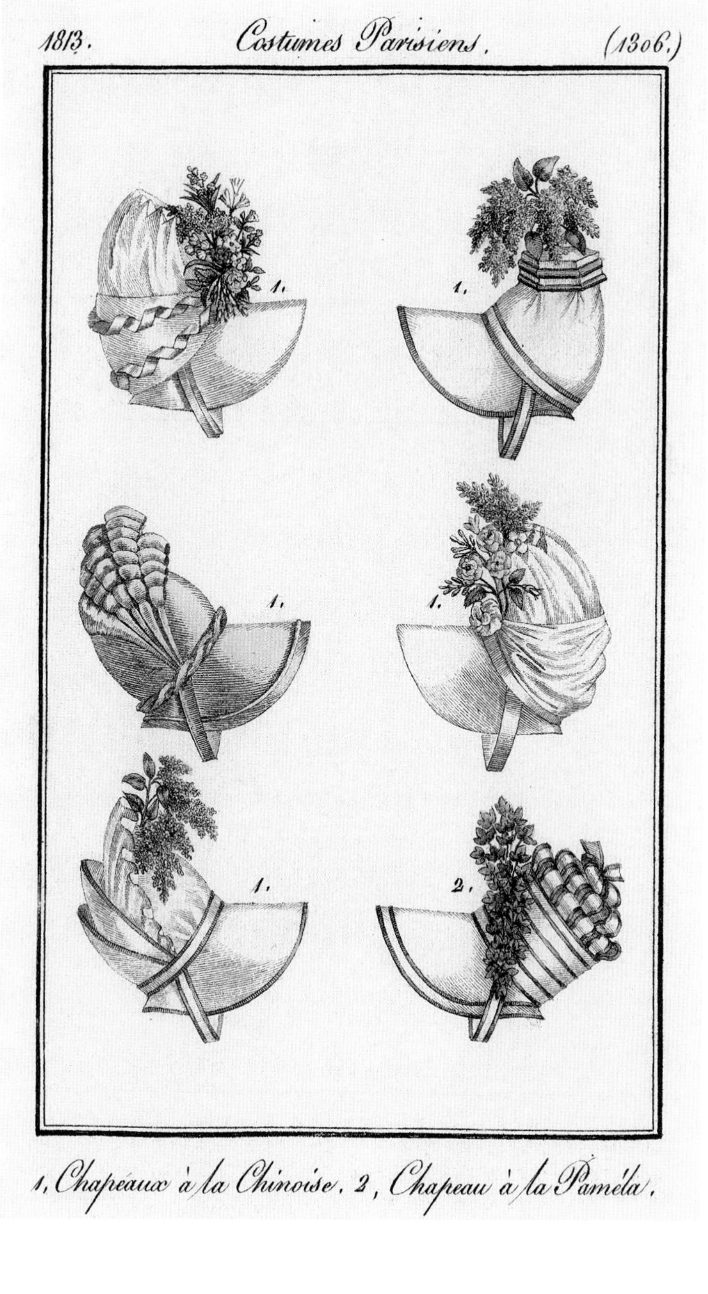
1813. Costumes Parisiens. (1306.)
1.
1.
1.
1.
1.
2.
1, Chapéaux à la Chinoise. 2, Chapeau à la Paméla.

Etching, 1813

Gravure, 1813

Radierung, 1813

Гравюра, Париж, 1813

Chapeaux de Gros de Naples.

Etching, 1813

Gravure, 1813

Radierung, 1813

Гравюра, Париж, 1813

Chapeau à la Jockey. Spencer de Lévantine.

Etching, 1813

Gravure, 1813

Radierung, 1813

Гравюра, Париж, 1813

1813.   *Costume Parisien.*

(1291.)

Chapeau de Velours épinglé. Redingote de Casimir.

Etching, 1813

Gravure, 1813

Radierung, 1813

Гравюра, Париж, 1813

1814. Costumes Parisiens. (1448.)

Etching, 1814

Gravure, 1814

Radierung, 1814

Гравюра, Париж, 1814

1, Chapeaux et Cornette de Velours plein. 2, Chapeau de Velours Chiné. 3, Chapeaux de Velours épinglé.

34

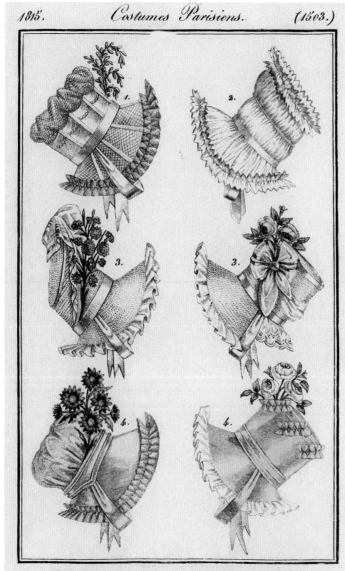

1, Chapeau de Gaze. 2, Capote de Perkale.
3, Chapeaux de paille. 4, Chapeaux de Gros de Naples.

Etching, 1815

Gravure, 1815

Radierung, 1815

Гравюра, Париж, 1815

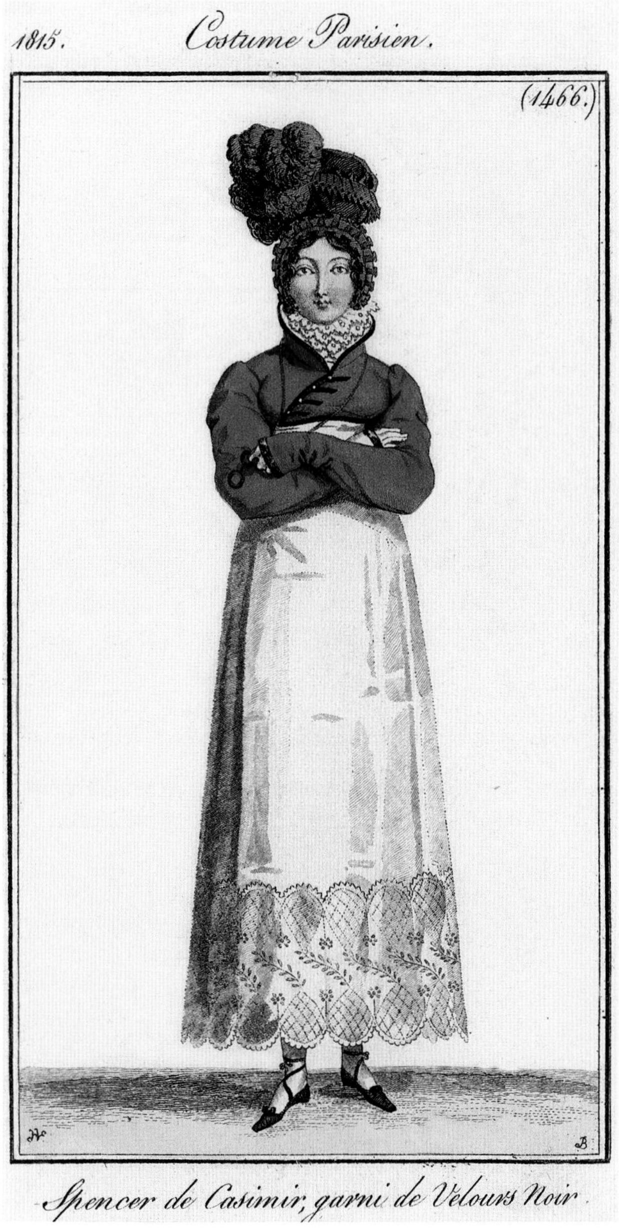
1815.
Costume Parisien.
(1466.)
Spencer de Casimir, garni de Velours Noir.

Etching, 1815

Gravure, 1815

Radierung, 1815

Гравюра, Париж, 1815

1815. *Costume Parisien.*

(1452.)

Chapeau de Velours épinglé. Witz-choura garni de petit Gris.

Etching, 1815

Gravure, 1815

Radierung, 1815

Гравюра, Париж, 1815

(1478.)

Capote de Gaze. Robe de Perkale.

Etching, 1815

Gravure, 1815

Radierung, 1815

Гравюра, Париж, 1815

(1465.)

Cornette en Coques de Rubans et en Blonde.
Redingote de Lévantine garnie de Velours chinalé.

Etching, 1815

Gravure, 1815

Radierung, 1815

Гравюра, Париж, 1815

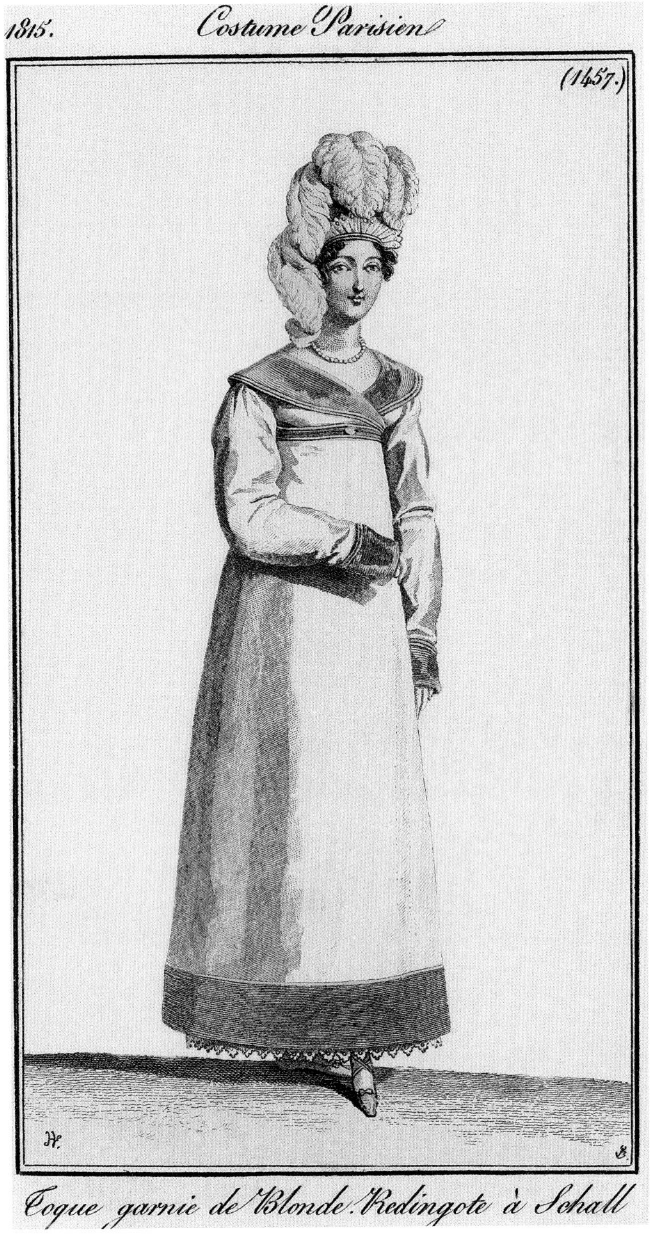
1815.
Costume Parisien
(1457.)
Toque garnie de Blonde. Redingote à Schall

Etching, 1815

Gravure, 1815

Radierung, 1815

Гравюра, Париж, 1815

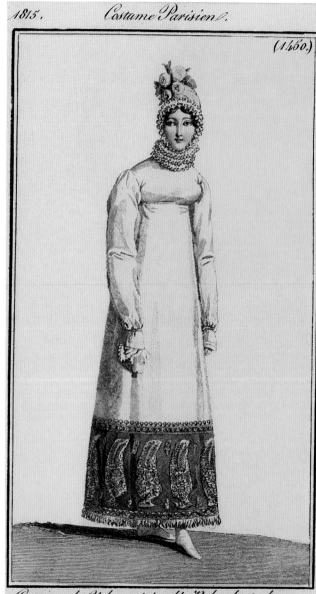

1815.   *Costume Parisien.*

(1450.)

Cornette de Velours épinglé. Robe de Cachemire.

Etching, 1815

Gravure, 1815

Radierung, 1815

Гравюра, Париж, 1815

Toque en diadême. Bas de Robe garni en Rubans.

Etching, 1815

Gravure, 1815

Radierung, 1815

Гравюра, Париж, 1815

1815.   *Costume Parisien.*

(1463.)

Chapeau de Velours. Robe de Velours garnie en Chenille.

Etching, 1815

Gravure, 1815

Radierung, 1815

Гравюра, Париж, 1815

Cornette de Perkale, Camisole et Robe de Perkale.

Etching, 1815

Gravure, 1815

Radierung, 1815

Гравюра, Париж, 1815

(1471.)

Robe et par-dessus de Levantine.

Etching, 1815

Gravure, 1815

Radierung, 1815

Гравюра, Париж, 1815

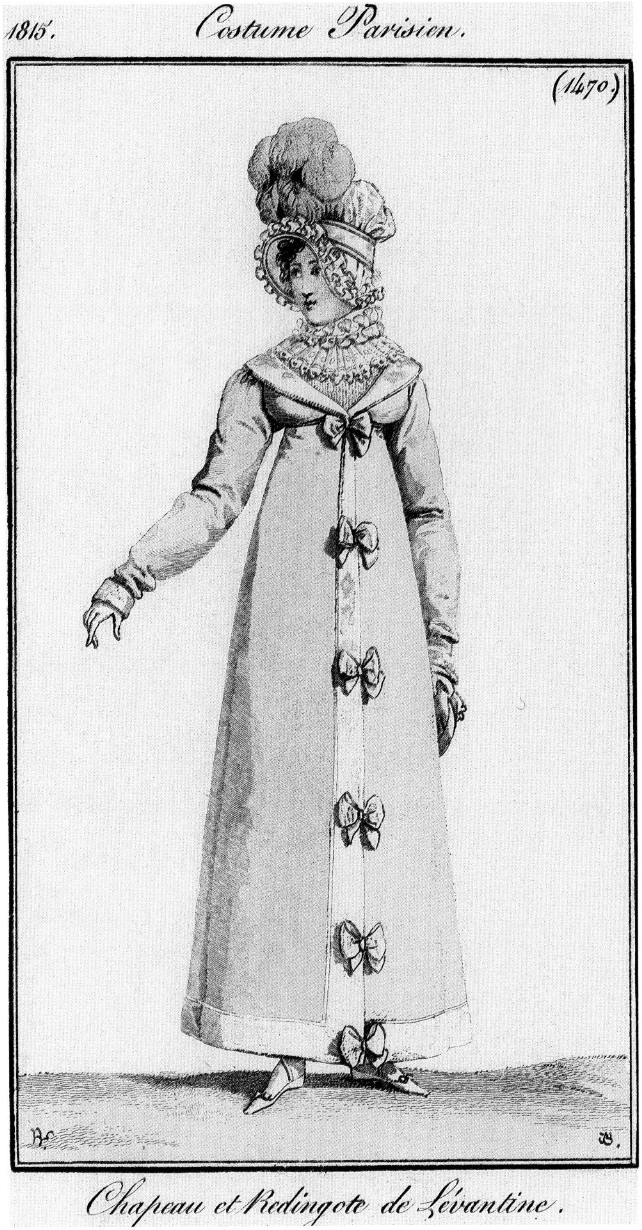
1815.
Costume Parisien.
(1470.)
Chapeau et Redingote de Lévantine.

Etching, 1815

Gravure, 1815

Radierung, 1815

Гравюра, Париж, 1815

1815.   *Costume Parisien*   (1486.)

Capote boiteuse. Fichu Ecossais.

Etching, 1815

Gravure, 1815

Radierung, 1815

Гравюра, Париж, 1815

1, *Chapeaux et Cornettes de Velours plein.*
2, *Chapeau de Velours épinglé et Satin.*

Etching, 1815

Gravure, 1815

Radierung, 1815

Гравюра, Париж, 1815

48

1, Toque de Velours épinglé. 2, Chapeaux de Velours épinglé.
3, Chapeau et Cornette de Velours plein.

Etching, 1815

Gravure, 1815

Radierung, 1815

Гравюра, Париж, 1815

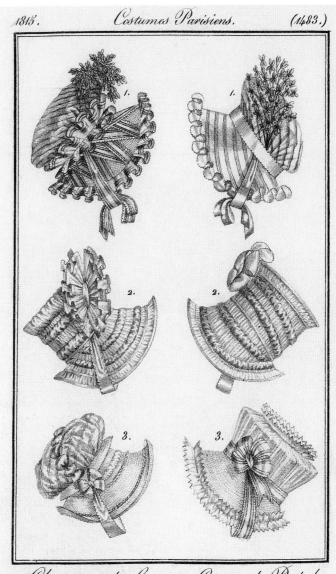

1, Chapeaux de Gaze. 2, Capotes de Perkale.
3, Chapeaux à fond de Gaze et passe de paille.

Etching, 1815

Gravure, 1815

Radierung, 1815

Гравюра, Париж, 1815

(1481.)

Fichu en Marmotte. Robe de Levantine.

Etching, 1815

Gravure, 1815

Radierung, 1815

Гравюра, Париж, 1815

1, *Chapeaux de Velours plein.* 2, *Chapeau de Satin et Gaze.*
3, *Toque de Velours plein.* 4, *Toque de Velours et Satin.*

Etching, 1816

Gravure, 1816

Radierung, 1816

Гравюра, Париж, 1816

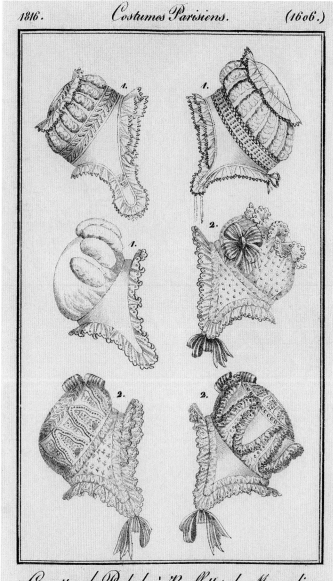

1, *Cornettes de Perkale à Bouffettes de Mousseline.*
2, *Cornettes de Mousseline Brodée.*

Etching, 1816

Gravure, 1816

Radierung, 1816

Гравюра, Париж, 1816

1, Chapeaux de paille. 2, Cornette de Mousseline brodée.
3, Capote de Perkale. 4, Chapeau de Crêpe.

Etching, 1817

Gravure, 1817

Radierung, 1817

Гравюра, Париж, 1817

54

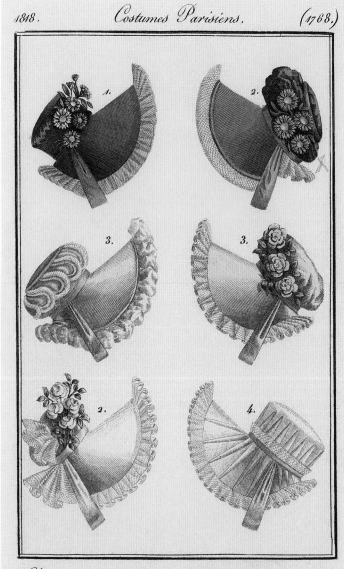

1, Chapeau de Gros de Naples. 2, Capotes de Gros de Naples.
3, Chapeaux de Crêpe. 4, Chapeau de Gros de Naples et Satin.

Etching, 1818

Gravure, 1818

Radierung, 1818

Гравюра, Париж, 1818

1818. *Costume Parisien.*

(1717.)

Robe de Satin, par-dessus de Tulle. Costume de Mariée.

Etching, 1818

Gravure, 1818

Radierung, 1818

Гравюра, Париж, 1818

Costumes Parisiens.

1818.

1. 2. (19.)

Etching, 1818

Gravure, 1818

Radierung, 1818

Гравюра, Париж, 1818

1818. *Costume Parisien.*

(1757.)

Capote écrue doublée de taffetas. Robe de Perkale garnie de bouillons et entredeux de Tulle.

Etching, 1818

Gravure, 1818

Radierung, 1818

Гравюра, Париж, 1818

1818.
Costume Parisien.
(1724.)

Chapeau de Gros de Naples. Robe de Tissu garnie de bouillons et ganses.

Etching, 1818

Gravure, 1818

Radierung, 1818

Гравюра, Париж, 1818

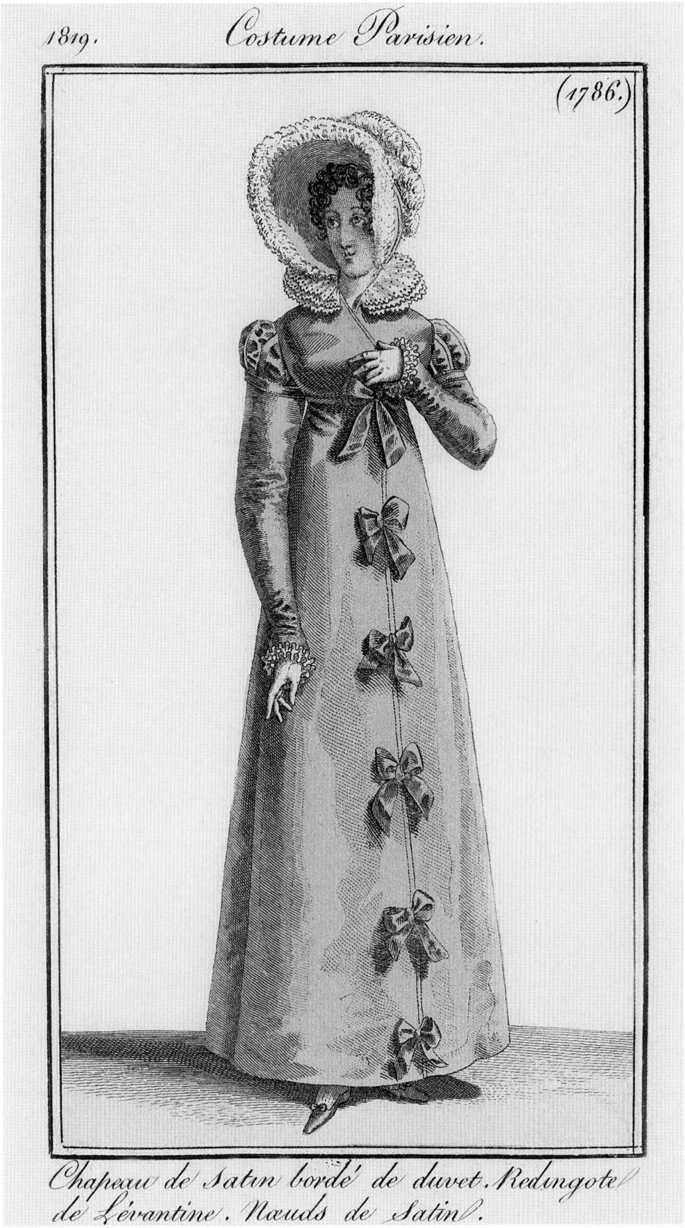
1819. Costume Parisien.
(1786.)
Chapeau de Satin bordé de duvet. Redingote de Lévantine. Nœuds de Satin.

Etching, 1819

Gravure, 1819

Radierung, 1819

Гравюра, Париж, 1819

1819.   *Costume Parisien.*

(1798.)

*Chapeau de Velours simulé, garni de duvet de Cygne. Robe de Mérinos,
à cœur, garnie de petit gris. Gibecière de Velours, garnie en acier.*

Etching, 1819

Gravure, 1819

Radierung, 1819

Гравюра, Париж, 1819

Chapeau de Castor garni d'une gance d'or
Robe de lévantine.

Etching, 1819

Gravure, 1819

Radierung, 1819

Гравюра, Париж, 1819

1819.   *Costume Parisien.*   *(1824.)*

Capote de Perkale. Echarpe de Baréges. Robe de Perkale garnie de mousseline.

Etching, 1819

Gravure, 1819

Radierung, 1819

Гравюра, Париж, 1819

1819.   *Costume Parisien.*

(1827.)

Etching, 1819

Gravure, 1819

Radierung, 1819

Гравюра, Париж, 1819

Chapeau de gros de Naples, orné de fleurs de Tulipier.
Robe de Batiste écrue, à Taille boutonnée. Fichu de Gaze.

64

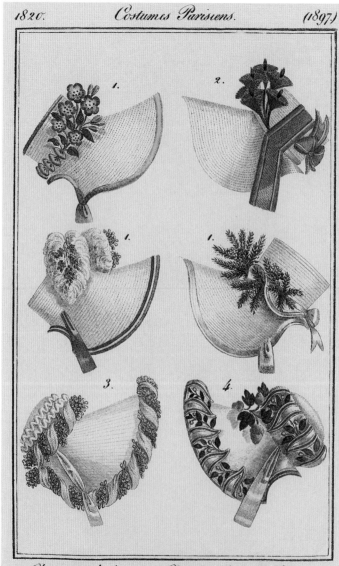

1. Chapeaux de bois. 2. Chapeau de lacets de coton.
3. Chapeau de crêpe. 4. Chapeau de gros de Naples,
avec des pattes de paille.

Etching, 1820

Gravure, 1820

Radierung, 1820

Гравюра, Париж, 1820

65

1, *Chapeaux de Crêpe.* 2, *Chapeaux de Gaze.*
3, *Chapeau de paille*

Etching, 1820

Gravure, 1820

Radierung, 1820

Гравюра, Париж, 1820

1840

1849

LA MODE

et coiffure de (Lemonnier Debuoy) Plumes de (Cartico fils) Etoffes de Robes et Pardessus de la M.ᵐᵉ Chambellan Faᵉ

Lithograph, Paris, 840 ca.

Lithographie, Paris,
vers 1840

Steindruck, Paris, gegen
das Jahr 1840

Литография, Париж, 1840

Lithograph, Paris, 1840 ca.

Lithographie,
Paris, vers 1840

Steindruck, Paris,
gegen das Jahr 1840

Литография, Париж, 1840

LA MODE

Travestissements

*Bonnet garni de Dentelles.
dessous Damas broché garni
de Velours. Jupes de dessous
de Satin*

*Toque de Velours garnie de Cygne.
Jupe de Satin garnie de petit
Velours. Pardessus de Velours orné
de Passementeries et de Cygne.*

LA MODE

Modes de Longchamps

Chapeaux de (Lemonnier Pelvey) Etoffes de robes du Pavillon d'Hanovre) façon de (M.lle de Moismont)
Mantelet de tulle brodé de (Richard Pottier) Gants (Mayer) Fauteuil de (Maigret) envois de la Maison
de Commission (Lassalle) 28, Taitbout.

Lithograph, Paris, 1840 ca.

Lithographie, Paris, vers 1840

Steindruck, Paris,
gegen das Jahr 1840

Литография, Париж, 1840

LA MODE

Lithograph, Paris, 1840 ca.

Lithographie, Paris, vers 1840

Steindruck, Paris,
gegen das Jahr 1840

Литография, Париж, 1840

LA MODE

Chapeaux de (Lemonnier-Pelsor) Etoffes de robes et Camail de Velours de (Gazelin-Opiger) Façon de robes de (M.lle de Moismont) Lingerie et Volant de Dentelle noire de (Doucet) Fourrure et Manchon de (Gou) Gants (Mayer) Mouchoir de (Chapron) Chaussures de (Beaudrand) Décors

Lithograph, Paris, 1846 ca.

Lithographie, Paris, vers 1846

Steindruck, Paris,
gegen das Jahr 1846

Литография, Париж, 1846

LA MODE

Robe de (Gazelin Opiger) façon de Robe de (Melle de Moismout) Fleurs de (Constantin) Gants (Mayer) Mouchoir de (Chapron) Mantelet de velours avec garniture de cygne de (Mallard) Console et Fauteuil de (Maigret) Ensemble de toilette expedié par la Maison de Commission (Lassalle) 28, Taitbout.

Lithograph, Paris, 1846 ca.

Lithographie, Paris,
vers 1846

Steindruck, Paris,
gegen das Jahr 1846

Литография, Париж, 1846

LA MODE

15 Juillet

Capote et Chapeau de (Mariton) 2 P.ᵈᵉ de la Madeleine Fleurs de (Constantin) Robes de (Mᵐᵉˢ Desfontaine
& Cᵉ) 2 Royale, Mouchoir de (Chapron Frᵉˢ) Gants (Mayer) Epingle de (Bou) Brodequins de (Baudrand) 340
S.ᵗ Honoré, Chaise de (Maiqret) toilette expédié par la Mᵒⁿ de Comᵒⁿ (Lassalle) 28. Taibout.

Lithograph, Paris, 1846 ca.

Lithographie, Paris, vers
1846

Steindruck, Paris,
gegen das Jahr 1846

Литография, Париж, 1846

LA MODE   25 Juillet

Chapeaux de (Lemonnier Delvey) 1. S.t honoré; Robes de (M.mes Desfontaines & C.ie) r. Royale, 25, Lingerie
(Doucet) de la Paix; Gants (Mayer) de la Paix; Brodequins de (Beaudrand) 348. S.t honoré; Ombrelle de
(Cazal) ensemble de toilette expédié par la M.on de Cou.re (Lassalle) 28, Taitbout.

à Paris, 28, Rue Taitbout (Chaussée d'Antin)

Lithograph, Paris, 1847 ca.

Lithographie, Paris,
vers 1847

Steindruck, Paris,
gegen das Jahr 1847

Литография, Париж, 1847

Lithograph, Paris, 1849
Lithographie, Paris, 1849
Steindruck, Paris, 1849
Литография, Париж, 1849

Dujardins   25 Décembre 1849.

MAGASIN DES DEMOISELLES.

1849

1850

MODE DEL GIORNO

Corriere delle Dame

30 Dicembre 1849   *Milano f.da S.Paolo 936*

Lithograph, Milan, 1849
Litographie, Milan, 1849
Steindruck, Mailand, 1849
Литография, Милан, 1849

Lithograph, Milan, 1849
Litographie, Milan, 1849
Steindruck, Mailand, 1849
Литография, Милан, 1849

MODE DI PARIGI

Corriere delle Dame

Lithograph, Milan, 1849
Litographie, Milan, 1849
Steindruck, Mailand, 1849
Литография, Милан, 1849

Mode di Parigi

Lithograph, *Milan, 1849*
Litographie, Milan, 1849
Steindruck, Mailand, 1849
Литография, Милан, 1849

Lithograph, Milan, 1849
Litographie, Milan, 1849
Steindruck, Mailand, 1849
Литография, Милан, 1849

MODE DI PARIGI

Corriere delle Dame

31 Dicembre 1850. Pl. 54.   Milano C.ta S. Paolo 936.

Lithograph, Milan, 1850
Litographie, Milan, 1850
Steindruck, Mailand, 1850
Литография, Милан, 1850

MODE DI PARIGI

Dicembre 1850.

Milano C. *S. Paolo* *936.*

Lithograph, Milan, 1850
Litographie, Milan, 1850
Steindruck, Mailand, 1850
Литография, Милан, 1850

Lithograph, *Gandini*, Corriere delle dame, *Milan, 1850*
Litographie, Gandini, *Corriere delle dame*, Milan, 1850
Steindruck, Gandini, *Corriere delle dame*, Mailand, 1850
Литография, Гандини, журнал «Corriere delle dame», Милан, 1850

MODE DI PARIGI

Corriere delle Dame

22 Ottobre 1850. N. 44.   Milano C. S. Paolo 936.

Lithograph, Milan, 1850
Litographie, Milan, 1850
Steindruck, Mailand, 1850
Литография, Милан, 1850

MODE DI PARIGI

Corriere delle Dame

3 Dicembre 1850. N.° 50.

Milano C.^{da} S. Paolo 936.

Lithograph, Milan, 1850
Litographie, Milan, 1850
Steindruck, Mailand, 1850
Литография, Милан, 1850

Lithograph, Milan, 1850
Litographie, Milan, 1850
Steindruck, Mailand, 1850
Литография, Милан, 1850

*Lithograph, italian fashion
Milan, 1850 ca.*

Litographie, mode
italienne, Milan,
vers 1850

Steindruck, italienisch
Mode, Mailand, gegen
das Jahr 1850

Литография, итальянская
мода, 1850

Lithograph, italian fashion Milan, 1850 ca.

Litographie, mode italienne, Milan, vers 1850

Steindruck, italienisch Mode, Mailand, gegen das Jahr 1850

Литография, итальянская мода, 1850

Lithograph, italian fashion Milan, 1850 ca.

Litographie, mode italienne, Milan, vers 1850

Steindruck, italienisch Mode, Mailand, gegen das Jahr 1850

Литография, итальянская мода, 1850

Lithograph, italian fashion Milan, 1850

Litographie, mode italienne, Milan, vers 1850

Steindruck, italienisch Mode, Mailand, gegen das Jahr 1850

Литография, итальянская мода, 1850

*Lithograph, italian
fashion Milan,
1850 ca.*

Litographie, mode
italienne, Milan,
vers 1850

Steindruck, italienisch
Mode, Mailand,
gegen das Jahr 1850

Литография,
итальянская мода,
1850

Lit. Vergnano   20

*Lithograph, italian
fashion Milan, 1850 ca.*

Litographie, mode
italienne, Milan,
vers 1850

Steindruck, italienisch
Mode, Mailand, gegen
das Jahr 1850

Литография,
итальянская мода, 1850

*Lithograph, italian fashion
Milan, 1850 ca.*

Litographie, mode italienne,
Milan, vers 1850

Steindruck, italienisch Mode,
Mailand, gegen das Jahr 1850

Литография,
итальянская мода, 1850

Lithograph, italian fashion Milan, 1850 ca.

Litographie, mode italienne, Milan, vers 1850

Steindruck, italienisch Mode, Mailand, gegen das Jahr 1850

Литография, итальянская мода, 1850

1854

1859

MAGASIN DES DEMOISELLES

Lithograph, Paris, 1854
Litographie, Paris, 1854
Steindruck, Paris, 1854
Литография, Париж, 1854

MAGASIN DES DEMOISELLES

Lithograph, Paris, 1855

Litographie, Paris, 1855

Steindruck, Paris, 1855

Литография, Париж, 1855

MAGASIN DES DEMOISELLES

Lithograph, Paris, 1855

Litographie, Paris, 1855

Steindruck, Paris, 1855

Литография, Париж, 1855

Lithograph, Paris, 1855
Litographie, Paris, 1855
Steindruck, Paris, 1855
Литография, Париж, 1855

MAGASIN DES DEMOISELLES

Lithograph, Paris, 1856
Lithographie, Paris, 1856
Steindruck, Paris, 1856
Литография, Париж, 1856

Lithograph, Paris, 1856
Lithographie, Parigi, 1856
Steindruck, Paris, 1856
Литография, Париж, 1856

eaux du Journal

MAGASIN DES DEMOISELL

12.ᵉannée   25 Mars 1856
51. rue Laffitte. Paris

Lithograph, Paris, 1856
Lithographie, Parigi, 1856
Steindruck, Paris, 1856
Литография, Париж, 1856

MAGASIN DES DEMOISELLES

Lithograph, Paris, 1857
Lithographie, Parigi, 1857
Steindruck, Paris, 1857
Литография, Париж, 1857

MAGASIN DES DEMOISELLES

Lithograph, Paris, 1857
Lithographie, Parigi, 1857
Steindruck, Paris, 1857
Литография, Париж, 1857

MAGASIN DES DEMOISELLES

Lithograph, Paris, 1859
Lithographie, Parigi, 1859
Steindruck, Paris, 1859
Литография, Париж, 1859

MAGASIN DES DEMOISELLES

Lithograph, Paris, 1859
Lithographie, Parigi, 1859
Steindruck, Paris, 1859
Литография, Париж, 1859

1860

1870

Journal des Demoiselles
Paris, Boulevart des Italiens, 1.

Lithograph, Paris, 1860 ca.
Lithographie, Paris, vers 1860
Steindruck, Paris, gegen das Jahr 1860
Литография, Париж, 1860

Lithograph, Paris, 1860
Lithographie, Paris, 1860
Steindruck, Paris, 1860
Литография, Париж, 1860

Lithograph, Paris, 1860 ca.
Lithographie, Paris, vers 1860
Steindruck, Paris, gegen das Jahr 1860
Литография, Париж, 1860

Lithograph, Paris, 1870
Litographie, Paris, 1870
Steindruck, Paris, 1870
Литография, Париж, 1870

Lithograph, Paris, 1870
Litographie, Paris, 1870
Steindruck, Paris, 1870
Литография, Париж, 1870

Lithograph, Paris, 1870
Litographie, Paris, 1870
Steindruck, Paris, 1870
Литография, Париж, 1870

Lithograph, Paris, 1870
Litographie, Paris, 1870
Steindruck, Paris, 1870
Литография, Париж, 1870

Lithograph, Paris, 1870
Litographie, Paris, 1870
Steindruck, Paris, 1870
Литография, Париж, 1870

Lithograph, Paris, 1870
Litographie, Paris, 1870
Steindruck, Paris, 1870
Литография, Париж, 1870

Lithograph, Paris, 1870
Litographie, Paris, 1870
Steindruck, Paris, 1870
Литография, Париж, 1870

Lithograph, Paris, 1870
Litographie, Paris, 1870
Steindruck, Paris, 1870
Литография, Париж, 1870

Lithograph, Paris, 1870
Litographie, Paris, 1870
Steindruck, Paris, 1870
Литография, Париж, 1870

Lithograph, Paris, 1870
Litographie, Paris, 1870
Steindruck, Paris, 1870
Литография, Париж, 1870

1876

1890

Lithograph, Paris, 1876
Lithographie, Paris, 1876
Steindruck, Paris, 1876
Литография, Париж, 1876

Lithograph, Paris, 1880 ca.

Lithographie,
Paris, vers 1880

Steindruck, Paris, gegen das
Jahr 1880

Литография, Париж, 1880

Lithograph, Paris, 1882
Lithographie, Paris, 1882
Steindruck, Paris, 1882
Литография, Париж, 1882

Lithograph, Paris, 1886 ca.

Lithographie, Paris, vers 1886

Steindruck, Paris, gegen das Jahr 1886

Литография, Париж, 1886

Lithograph, Paris, 1886 ca.

Lithographie, Paris, vers 1886

Steindruck, Paris, gegen das Jahr 1886

Литография, Париж, 1886

Journal des Demoiselles
ET PETIT COURRIER DES DAMES RÉUNIS

Lithograph, Paris, 1886 ca.

Lithographie, Paris, vers 1886

Steindruck, Paris, gegen das Jahr 1886

Литография, Париж, 1886

Lithograph, Paris, 1886 ca.

Lithographie, Paris, vers 1886

Steindruck, Paris, gegen das Jahr 1886

Литография, Париж, 1886

Lithograph, Paris, 1889
Lithographie, Paris, 1889
Steindruck, Paris, 1889
Литография, Париж, 1889

Modes de Paris
Journal des Demoiselles
Paris, Boulevart des Italiens. 1.

Lithograph, Paris, 1890 ca.
Lithographie, Paris, vers 1890
Steindruck, Paris, gegen das Jahr 1890
Литография, Париж, 1890

Lithograph, Paris, 1890 ca.
Lithographie, Paris, vers 1890
Steindruck, Paris, gegen das Jahr 1890
Литография, Париж, 1890

Lithograph, Paris, 1890 ca.
Lithographie, Paris, vers 1890
Steindruck, Paris, gegen das Jahr 1890
Литография, Париж, 1890

Journal des Demoiselles

Lithograph, Paris, 1890 ca.
Lithographie, Paris, vers 1890
Steindruck, Paris, gegen das Jahr 1890
Литография, Париж, 1890

Journal des Demoiselles

Lithograph, Paris, 1890 ca.
Lithographie, Paris, vers 1890
Steindruck, Paris, gegen das Jahr 1890
Литография, Париж, 1890

Journal des Demoiselles

Paris, Boulevart des Italiens.

Lithograph, Paris, 1890 ca.
Lithographie, Paris, vers 1890
Steindruck, Paris, gegen das Jahr 1890
Литография, Париж, 1890

Lithograph, Paris, 1890 ca.
Lithographie, Paris, vers 1890
Steindruck, Paris, gegen das Jahr 1890
Литография, Париж, 1890

Journal des Demoiselles
Paris. Boulevart des Italiens .1.

Lithograph, Paris, 1890 ca.
Lithographie, Paris, vers 1890
Steindruck, Paris, gegen das Jahr 1890
Литография, Париж, 1890

Journal des Demoiselles

Paris. Boulevart des Italiens 1.

Lithograph, Paris, 1890 ca.
Lithographie, Paris, vers 1890
Steindruck, Paris, gegen das Jahr 1890
Литография, Париж, 1890

Lithograph, Paris, 1890 ca.
Lithographie, Paris, vers 1890
Steindruck, Paris, gegen das Jahr 1890
Литография, Париж, 1890

Journal des Demoiselles

Lithograph, Paris, 1890 ca.
Lithographie, Paris, vers 1890
Steindruck, Paris, gegen das Jahr 1890
Литография, Париж, 1890

Journal des Demoiselles
Paris, Boulevard des Italiens

Lithograph, Paris, 1890
Lithographie, Paris, 1890
Steindruck, Paris, 1890
Литография, Париж, 1890

Journal des Demoiselles

Paris, Boulevart des Italiens, 1.

Lithograph, Paris, 1890 ca.
Lithographie, Paris, vers 1890
Steindruck, Paris, gegen das Jahr 1890
Литография, Париж, 1890

Journal des Demoiselles

Lithograph, Paris, 1890 ca.
Lithographie, Paris, vers 1890
Steindruck, Paris, gegen das Jahr 1890
Литография, Париж, 1890

Journal des Demoiselles

Lithograph, Paris, 1890 ca.
Lithographie, Paris, vers 1890
Steindruck, Paris, gegen das Jahr 1890
Литография, Париж, 1890

Lithograph, Paris, 1890 ca.
Lithographie, Paris, vers 1890
Steindruck, Paris, gegen das Jahr 1890
Литография, Париж, 1890

Lithograph, Paris, 1890 ca.

Lithographie, Paris, vers 1890

Steindruck, Paris, gegen das Jahr 1890

Литография, Париж, 1890

Lithograph, Paris, 1890 ca.

Lithographie, Paris, vers 1890

Steindruck, Paris, gegen das Jahr 1890

Литография, Париж, 1890

Lithograph, Paris, 1890 ca.

Lithographie, Paris,
vers 1890

Steindruck, Paris, gegen das
Jahr 1890

Литография, Париж, 1890

Lithograph, Paris, 1890 ca.

Lithographie, Paris, vers 1890

Steindruck, Paris, gegen das
Jahr 1890

Литография, Париж, 1890

Lithograph, Paris, 1890 ca.

Lithographie, Paris, vers 1890

Steindruck, Paris, gegen das Jahr 1890

Литография, Париж, 1890

Lithograph, Paris, 1890 ca.

Lithographie, Paris,
vers 1890

Steindruck, Paris, gegen
das Jahr 1890

Литография, Париж, 1890

Journal des Demoiselles

Modes de Paris.   ET PETIT COURRIER DES DAMES RÉUNIS   Rue Vivienne. 48.

Toilettes de Mlles VIDAL 104 r. de Richelieu-Chapeaux de Mme BOUCHERIE 16 r. du Vieux Colombier
Véloutine FAY 9 r. de la Paix-Éventails de la Mon KEES 28 r. du 4 Septembre.

4563

Juurnal des Demoiselles

Modes de Paris. ET PETIT COURRIER DES DAMES RÉUNIS Rue Vivienne 48.

Toilettes de Mme TURLE 3 r. de Clichy Chapeaux de Mme BOUCHERIE 16 r. du Vieux Colombier.
Etoffes brodées de la Mon d'ANTHOINE — Ceinture Regente et Corset Anne d'Autriche de la

Lithograph, Paris, 1890 ca.

Lithographie, Paris,
vers 1890

Steindruck, Paris, gegen das
Jahr 1890

Литография, Париж, 1890

Lithograph, Paris, 1890 ca.

Lithographie, Paris, vers 1890

Steindruck, Paris, gegen das Jahr 1890

Литография, Париж, 1890

Journal des Demoiselles

Modes de Paris. ET PETIT COURRIER DES DAMES RÉUNIS Rue Vivienne, 48.

Lithograph, Paris, 1890 ca.

Lithographie, Paris,
vers 1890

Steindruck, Paris, gegen das
Jahr 1890

Литография, Париж, 1890

Lithograph, Paris, 1890 ca.

Lithographie, Paris,
vers 1890

Steindruck, Paris, gegen
das Jahr 1890

Литография, Париж, 1890

Journal des Demoiselles

ET PETIT COURRIER DES DAMES RÉUNIS

Modes de Paris   Rue Vivienne 48

4560

Lithograph, Paris, 1890 ca.

Lithographie, Paris, vers 1890

Steindruck, Paris, gegen das Jahr 1890

Литография, Париж, 1890

Lithograph, Paris, 1890 ca.

Lithographie, Paris, vers 1890

Steindruck, Paris, gegen das Jahr 1890

Литография, Париж, 1890

Lithograph, Paris, 1890 ca.

Lithographie, Paris, vers 1890

Steindruck, Paris, gegen das Jahr 1890

Литография, Париж, 1890

Lithograph, Paris, 1890 ca.

Lithographie, Paris, vers 1890

Steindruck, Paris, gegen das Jahr 1890

Литография, Париж, 1890

Lithograph, Paris, 1890 ca.

Lithographie, Paris, vers 1890

Steindruck, Paris, gegen das Jahr 1890

Литография, Париж, 1890

LA MODE ILLUSTRÉE

Bureaux du Journal 56 rue Jacob Paris

Chapeaux de Madame AUBERT, 34 r de la Victoire

Lithograph, Paris, 1890 ca.

Lithographie, Paris, vers 1890

Steindruck, Paris, gegen das
Jahr 1890

Литография, Париж, 1890

Journal des Demoiselles

Modes de Paris. ET PETIT COURRIER DES DAMES RÉUNIS Rue Vivienne. 48.

Lithograph, Paris, 1890 ca.

Lithographie, Paris,
vers 1890

Steindruck, Paris, gegen das
Jahr 1890

Литография, Париж, 1890

1919

Lithograph, Paris, 1919
Lithographie, Paris, 1919
Steindruck, Paris, 1919
Литография, Париж, 1919

LES ELEGANCES PARISIENNES

POUR L'HIVER

Lithograph, Paris, 1919
Lithographie, Paris, 1919
Steindruck, Paris, 1919
Литография, Париж, 1919

LES ÉLÉGANCES PARISIENNES

QUELQUES EMPLOIS DE RUBANS

Lithograph, Paris, 1919
Lithographie, Paris, 1919
Steindruck, Paris, 1919
Литография, Париж, 1919

LES ÉLÉGANCES PARISIENNES

TROIS TAILLEURS NOUVEAUX

Lithograph, Paris, 1919
Lithographie, Paris, 1919
Steindruck, Paris, 1919
Литография, Париж, 1919

Lithograph, Paris, 1919
Lithographie, Paris, 1919
Steindruck, Paris, 1919
Литография, Париж, 1919

APRÈS-MIDI ET PETIT SOIR

Lithograph, Paris, 1919
Lithographie, Paris, 1919
Steindruck, Paris, 1919
Литография, Париж, 1919

1922

RÊVEUSE

Pochoir, G.P. Joumard,
Paris, 1922

Pochoir,
G.P. Joumard,
Paris, 1922

Schlablone, G.P. Joumard,
Paris, 1922

Пошер,
G.P. Joumard,
Париж, 1922

Pochoir, G.P. Joumard,
Paris, 1922

Pochoir,
G.P. Joumard,
Paris, 1922

Schlablone, G.P. Joumard,
Paris, 1922

Пошер,
G.P. Joumard,
Париж, 1922

PROMENEUSE

CROISETTE

Pochoir, G.P. Joumard,
Paris, 1922

Pochoir,
G.P. Joumard,
Paris, 1922

Schlablone, G.P. Joumard,
Paris, 1922

Пошер, G.P. Joumard,
Париж, 1922

Pochoir, G.P. Joumard,
Paris, 1922

Pochoir,
G.P. Joumard,
Paris, 1922

Schlablone, G.P. Joumard,
Paris, 1922

Пошер, G.P. Joumard,
Париж, 1922

CHOUKY

MOUNA

Pochoir, G.P. Joumard,
Paris, 1922

Pochoir,
G.P. Joumard,
Paris, 1922

Schlablone, G.P. Joumard,
Paris, 1922

Пошер, G.P. Joumard,
Париж, 1922

Pochoir, G.P. Joumard,
Paris, 1922

Pochoir,
G.P. Joumard,
Paris, 1922

Schlablone, G.P. Joumard,
Paris, 1922

Пошер, G.P. Joumard,
Париж, 1922

LYNDA

TAMARIS

Pochoir, G.P. Joumard,
Paris, 1922

Pochoir,
G.P. Joumard,
Paris, 1922

Schlablone, G.P. Joumard,
Paris, 1922

Пошер, G.P. Joumard,
Париж, 1922

Pochoir, G.P. Joumard,
Paris, 1922

Pochoir,
G.P. Joumard,
Paris, 1922

Schlablone, G.P. Joumard,
Paris, 1922

Пошер, G.P. Joumard,
Париж, 1922

MANON

CÔTE-D'ARGENT.

Pochoir, G.P. Joumard,
Paris, 1922

Pochoir,
G.P. Joumard,
Paris, 1922

Schlablone, G.P. Joumard,
Paris, 1922

Пошер, G.P. Joumard,
Париж, 1922

Pochoir, G.P. Joumard,
Paris, 1922

Pochoir,
G.P. Joumard,
Paris, 1922

Schlablone, G.P. Joumard,
Paris, 1922

Пошер, G.P. Joumard,
Париж, 1922

BIJOU

FLEUR D'ARGENT

Pochoir, G.P. Joumard,
Paris, 1922

Pochoir,
G.P. Joumard,
Paris, 1922

Schlablone, G.P. Joumard,
Paris, 1922

Пошер, G.P. Joumard,
Париж, 1922

Pochoir, G.P. Joumard,
Paris, 1922

Pochoir,
G.P. Joumard,
Paris, 1922

Schlablone, G.P. Joumard,
Paris, 1922

Пошер, G.P. Joumard,
Париж, 1922

ALMÉE

MIRAGE

Pochoir, G.P. Joumard,
Paris, 1922

Pochoir,
G.P. Joumard,
Paris, 1922

Schlablone, G.P. Joumard,
Paris, 1922

Пошер, G.P., Joumard,
Париж, 1922

Pochoir, G.P. Joumard,
Paris, 1922

Pochoir,
G.P. Joumard,
Paris, 1922

Schlablone, G.P. Joumard,
Paris, 1922

Пошер, G.P. Joumard,
Париж, 1922

DISEUSE

BLUE

Pochoir, G.P. Joumard,
Paris, 1922

Pochoir,
G.P. Joumard,
Paris, 1922

Schlablone, G.P. Joumard,
Paris, 1922

Пошер, G.P., Joumard,
Париж, 1922

1938

les Créations Parisiennes

Nᵒˢ 150-151 - "Belami" est un charmant tailleur de lainage marine, porté avec une blouse de dentelle et georgette.

MARTIAL & ARMAND

Lithograph, Paris, 1938

Lithographie, Paris, 1938

Steindruck, Paris, 1938

Литография, Париж, 1938

les Créations Parisiennes

Lithograph, Paris, 1938

Lithographie, Paris, 1938

Steindruck, Paris, 1938

Литография, Париж, 1938

Nº 909. - *Robe en crêpe fantaisie présentant un effet de découpes croisées se terminant par un noué devant.*

Nº 910. - *En Tortaz noir cette charmante robe est travaillée de découpes arrondies de formes très nouvelles (tissu LESUR).*

909

910

Les Créations Parisiennes

Nº 100 - " Colombe. "
*Robe du soir en satin blanc
dont la jupe est plissée.
Petits boutons de glace.*

Nº 101 - " Pélagie. " *Robe
de cérémonie exécutée en
fine dentelle noire garnie
d'applications de tulle.*

100   101

Lithograph, Paris, 1938

Lithographie, Paris, 1938

Steindruck, Paris, 1938

Литография, Париж, 1938

les Créations Parisiennes

Lithograph, Paris, 1938

Lithographie, Paris, 1938

Steindruck, Paris, 1938

Литография, Париж, 1938

Nº 384 - *Elégante robe de crêpe mousse, ouvragée d'incrustations. Large ceinture drapée en longs pans.*

Nº 385 - *Manteau d'après midi, en ottoman noir étoffé de grands revers gracieusement torsadés*

384   385

les Créations Parisiennes

Nos 18-19 - *En crêpe d'albène corinthe, cette robe d'après-midi ouvragée d'effets de drapés maintenus sous des motifs de ganses blanches est portée sous un manteau de lainage de même ton enrichi de renard.*

18   19

Lithograph, Paris, 1938

Lithographie, Paris, 1938

Steindruck, Paris, 1938

Литография, Париж, 1938

les Créations Parisiennes

N°172 - Manteau d'après-midi en Katchouka réchauffé d'astrakan (Tissu LESUR).

N°173 - Robe en crêpe mousse garnie de piqures gansées et d'une ceinture nouée.

172

173

Lithograph, Paris, 1938

Lithographie, Paris, 1938

Steindruck, Paris, 1938

Литография, Париж, 1938

Les Créations Parisiennes

N° 407 - " Rallye
Ballon ". *Charmant
tailleur en lainage
marine incrusté de
manifyl de tons vifs.*

N° 408 - " Porte Dauphine ".
*Robe en jersey violet éclairée
de piqué blanc et se portant
avec une veste pied-de-poule,
représentée sur notre couverture.*

407   408

LUCILE MANGUIN

Lithograph, Paris, 1938

Lithographie, Paris, 1938

Steindruck, Paris, 1938

Литография, Париж, 1938

Les Créations Parisiennes

N° 65 - "Oust". Elégant tailleur de velours uni et côtelé; les gants et le chapeau sont assortis.

N° 66 - "Drags". Une opposition se combine dans cet élégant manteau de drap garni d'astrakan.

65   66

JACQUES HEIM

Lithograph, Paris, 1938

Lithographie, Paris, 1938

Steindruck, Paris, 1938

Литография, Париж, 1938

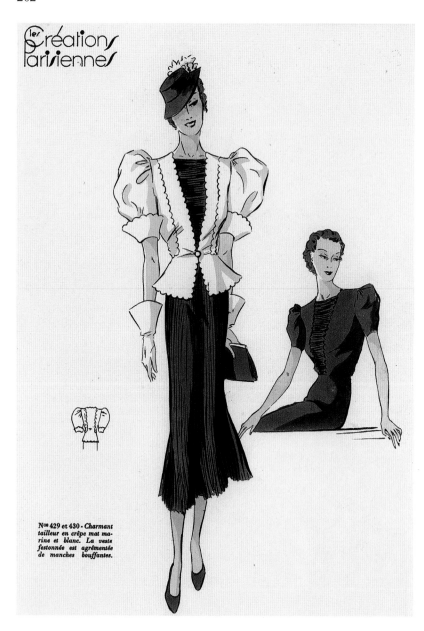

Créations Parisiennes

Nos 429 et 430 - *Charmant tailleur en crêpe mat marine et blanc. La veste festonnée est agrémentée de manches bouffantes.*

Lithograph, Paris, 1938

Lithographie, Paris, 1938

Steindruck, Paris, 1938

Литография, Париж, 1938

les Créations Parisiennes

Nos 24-25 - En fin lainage bleu-gris, cette robe est incrustée de velours ; un manteau de lainage du ton, orné d'astrakan noir l'accompagne.

24

25

Lithograph, Paris, 1938

Lithographie, Paris, 1938

Steindruck, Paris, 1938

Литография, Париж, 1938

Les Créations Parisiennes

227

Nᵒˢ 227-227 bis - *La Fermeture F. A. M. permet de transformer complètement cette robe d'après-midi en crêpe mat.*

227 bis

Lithograph, Paris, 1938

Lithographie, Paris, 1938

Steindruck, Paris, 1938

Литография, Париж, 1938

Création Parisiennes

Lithograph, Paris, 1938

Lithographie, Paris, 1938

Steindruck, Paris, 1938

Литография, Париж, 1938

N° 336. - *Charmant ensemble en duvetine, dont la veste vague est appliquée devant par une ceinture de daim brun.*

N° 337. - *Très pratique, cette petite robe en kasha naturel, dont le corsage est agrémenté de découpes.*

les Créations Parisiennes

Nº 730 - *Costume sport
composé de lainage uni
et lainage fantaisie.*

Nº 731 - *Cette charmante
robe est exécutée en lainage
chiné, ceinturée de cuir.*

730

731

Lithograph, Paris, 1938

Lithographie, Paris, 1938

Steindruck, Paris, 1938

Литография, Париж, 1938

les Créations Parisiennes

Nº 489 - " Zouzou. "
Deux-pièces en lainage
noir et quadrillé jaune et
noirceinturé de cuir verni.

Nº 490 - "Rosine." Une petite cape de lainage uni com-
plète une robe de lainage imprimé de pois verts et bruns.

489   490

MARTIAL & ARMAND

Lithograph, Paris, 1938

Lithographie, Paris, 1938

Steindruck, Paris, 1938

Литография, Париж, 1938

les Créations Parisiennes

No 156 - Une étroite tunique brodée de métal est portée sur une jupe de même crêpe mat.

No 157 - Le corsage très froncé de cette robe d'après-midi s'agrémente de deux petits jabots.

156

157

Lithograph, Paris, 1938

Lithographie, Paris, 1938

Steindruck, Paris, 1938

Литография, Париж, 1938

Les Créations Parisiennes

Nᵒˢ 164-165 - " Belle Sauvage ". *Robe de lainage noir, ceinturée de daim vert, portée sous un trois-quarts de même lainage étoffé de lynx.*

164   165

LUCILE MANGUIN

Lithograph, Paris, 1938

Lithographie, Paris, 1938

Steindruck, Paris, 1938

Литография, Париж, 1938

les Créations Parisiennes

Nº 16 - Charmante robe d'après-midi en crêpe noir ouvragée de fines nervures et égayée de fleurs et de biais roses.

Nº 17 - Plus simple cette robe de crêpe fantaisie noir est éclairée d'un col et de parements blancs.

16   17

LUCILE PARAY ET JENNY

Lithograph, Paris, 1938

Lithographie, Paris, 1938

Steindruck, Paris, 1938

Литография, Париж, 1938

les **Créations Parisiennes**

Nº 370 - *Petite robe d'une élégante simplicité en Kalkaz et garnie de velours* (Tissu LESUR).

Nº 371 - *En fin lainage, très chic modèle présente nouvel effet d'incrustatio*

Lithograph, Paris, 1938

Lithographie, Paris, 1938

Steindruck, Paris, 1938

Литография, Париж, 1938

les Créations Parisiennes

N° 593 - *Petite robe sans manches agrémentée de motifs de soutaches lavables bleu vif.*

N° 594 - *Charmante robe de plage boutonnée, exécutée en "Flocor" (Tissu RODIER)*

593   594

Lithograph, Paris, 1938

Lithographie, Paris, 1938

Steindruck, Paris, 1938

Литография, Париж, 1938

les Créations Parisiennes

Lithograph, Paris, 1938

Lithographie, Paris, 1938

Steindruck, Paris, 1938

Литография, Париж, 1938

N° 162 - Manteau d'après-midi en Nattaz orné d'astrakan (Tissu LESUR).

N° 163 - De petits volants d'organdi blanc éclairent cette robe d'après-midi en crêpe d'albène.

162

163

les Créations Parisiennes

Nº 174 - Cette élégante robe
d'après-midi simule un bo-
léro bordé de soutaches d'or.

174

Nº 175 - Des galons mai
tiennent les fronces de ce
robe de crêpe d'Albè

175

Lithograph, Paris, 1938

Lithographie, Paris, 1938

Steindruck, Paris, 1938

Литография, Париж, 1938

Les Créations Parisiennes

Lithograph, Paris, 1938

Lithographie, Paris, 1938

Steindruck, Paris, 1938

Литография, Париж, 1938

N° 502 - *Deux-pièces en toile de lin rose pâle dont la jupe est élargie d'un pli creux.*

N° 503 - *Elégant manteau en tortaz beige (Tissu LESUR) orné de découpes gansées.*

502

503

Créations
Parisiennes

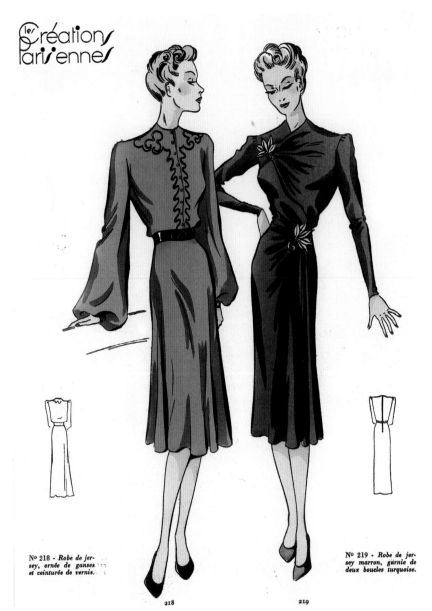

Nº 218 - Robe de jer-
sey, ornée de ganses
et ceinturée de vernis.

Nº 219 - Robe de jer-
sey marron, garnie de
deux boucles turquoise.

218

219

Lithograph, Paris, 1938

Lithographie, Paris, 1938

Steindruck, Paris, 1938

Литография, Париж, 1938

Lithograph, Paris, 1938

Lithographie, Paris, 1938

Steindruck, Paris, 1938

Литография, Париж, 1938

Les Créations Parisiennes

Nº 409 - Très printanier ce tailleur en crêpe mat uni et imprimé, fermé par des petits nœuds.

Nº 410 - Un souple lainage compose ce tailleur largement échancré sur une blouse d'organdi.

les Créations Parisiennes

Nº 431 - Tailleur brun en lainage uni et fantaisie. La jupe est élargie de plis.

Nº 432 - Confortable manteau en tortaz (tissu Lesur) brun roux, garni de boutons de cuir.

Lithograph, Paris, 1938

Lithographie, Paris, 1938

Steindruck, Paris, 1938

Литография, Париж, 1938

crêpe satin imprimé

Lithograph, Idées*, Paris, 1938*

Lithographie, *Idées*, Paris, 1938

Steindruck, *Idées*, Paris, 1938

Литография, *Idées*, Париж, 1938

crêpe satin

et anneaux
en métal
doré

crêpe mousse.
imprimé

Lithograph, Idées, *Paris, 1938*

Lithographie, *Idées*, Paris, 1938

Steindruck, *Idées*, Paris, 1938

Литография, *Idées*, Париж, 1938

dentelle de fil épaisse.

crêpe de soie

Lithograph, Idées*, Paris, 1938*

Lithographie, *Idées*, Paris, 1938

Steindruck, *Idées*, Paris, 1938

Литография, *Idées*, Париж, 1938

plastron en toile d'albène

jersey de laine

Lithograph, Idées, Paris, 1938

Lithographie, Idées, Paris, 1938

Steindruck, Idées, Paris, 1938

Литография, *Idées*, Париж, 1938

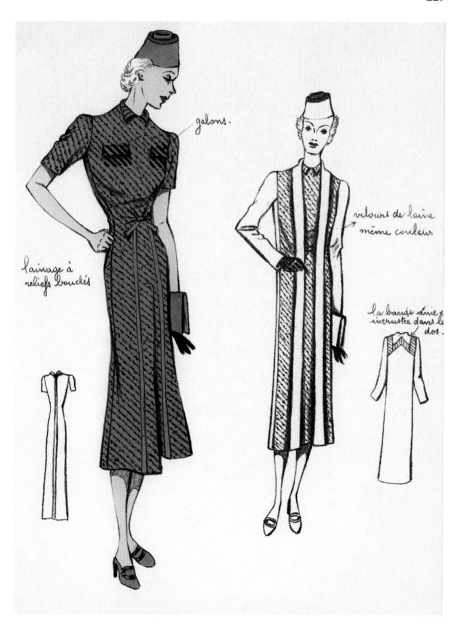

Lithograph, Idées, *Paris, 1938*

Lithographie, *Idées,* Paris, 1938

Steindruck, *Idées,* Paris, 1938

Литография, *Idées,* Париж, 1938

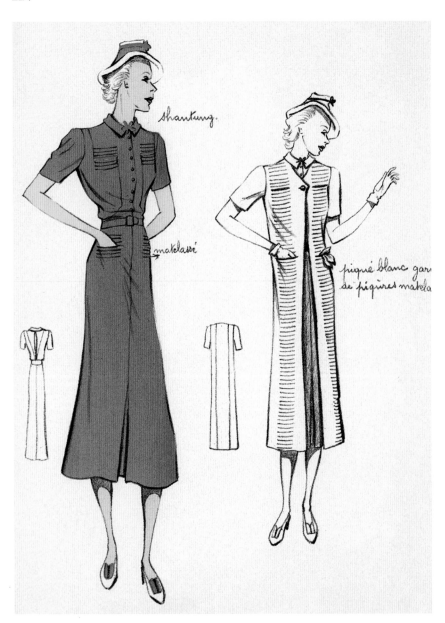

shantung.

matelassé

piqué blanc gar...
de piqûres matela...

Lithograph, Editions Idées,
Paris, 1938

Lithographie, Éditions
Idées, Paris, 1938

Steindruck, Editions Idées,
Paris, 1938

Литография, Editions
Idées, Париж, 1938

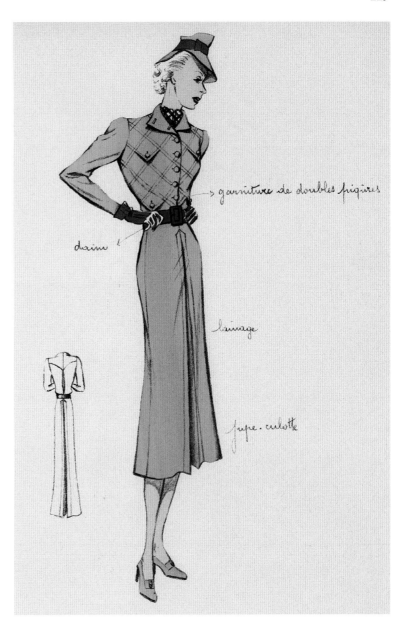

Lithograph, Idées*, Paris, 1938*

Lithographie, *Idées*, Paris, 1938

Steindruck, *Idées*, Paris, 1938

Литография, *Idées*, Париж, 1938

le col châle se
ferme dans le dos

gros grain

piqures
matelassées

Lithograph, Editions Idées, Paris, 1938

Lithographie, Éditions Idées, Paris, 1938

Steindruck, Editions Idées, Paris, 1938

Литография, Editions Idées, Париж, 1938

lainage angora écossais.

Lithograph, Idées*, Paris, 1938*

Lithographie, *Idées*, Paris, 1938

Steindruck, *Idées*, Paris, 1938

Литография, *Idées*, Париж, 1938

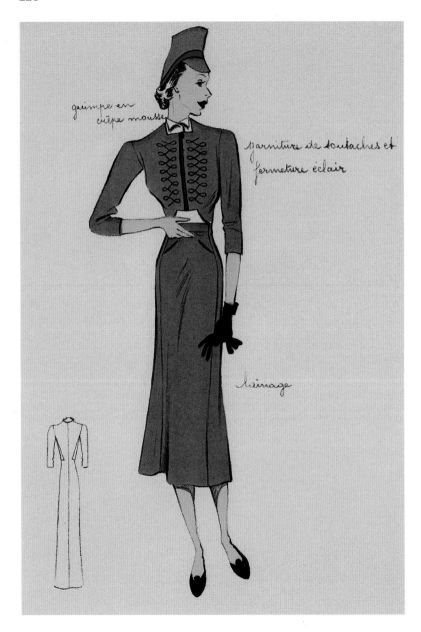

Lithograph, Idées*, Paris, 1938*

Lithographie, *Idées*, Paris, 1938

Steindruck, *Idées*, Paris, 1938

Литография, *Idées*, Париж, 1938

dain à incrustation de tissu

kasha

plis piqués.

1954

Autotipy, Saes, Milan, 1954

Autotypie, Saes, Milano, 1954

Autotypie, Saes, Mailand, 1954

Изд.Saes, Милан, 1954

Autotipy, Saes, Milan, 1954

Autotypie, Saes, Milano, 1954

Autotypie, Saes, Mailand, 1954

Изд.Saes, Милан, 1954

ARBITER

ARBITER

Autotipy, Saes, Milan, 1954

Autotypie, Saes, Milano, 1954

Autotypie, Saes, Mailand, 1954

Изд.Saes, Милан, 1954

Autotipy, Saes, Milan, 1954

Autotypie, Saes, Milano, 1954

Autotypie, Saes, Mailand, 1954

Изд.Saes, Милан, 1954

ARBITER

Autotipy, Saes, Milan, 1954

Autotypie, Saes, Milano, 1954

Autotypie, Saes, Mailand, 1954

Изд.Saes, Милан, 1954

Autotipy, Saes, Milan, 1954

Autotypie, Saes, Milano,
1954

Autotypie, Saes, Mailand,
1954

Изд.Saes, Милан, 1954

ARBITER